W9-AAC-980

Dear Students,

      Hi there, it's me Hardy Heart®. I'm all pumped up about kids learning to live a healthy lifestyle. This book is yours to use along with my Hardy Heart kit, Calci M. Bone®'s kit and Windy® the Lung's Kit. Not only will you be learning about good health, but you will also be doing math, science, language arts and other important smart stuff! Fill in your name below and get ready to have some fun!

Sincerely,

Hardy Heart

Hardy Heart

P.S. I left some room for you to draw a picture of yourself marching next to me.

_____

- -

_____
Name

Visit our web site at www.organwiseguys.com

HARDY HEART®'S KIT:

School Days Here We Come!

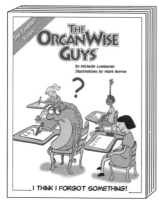

I Think I Forgot Something!

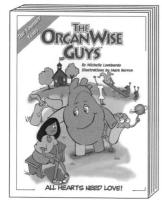

All Hearts Need Love!

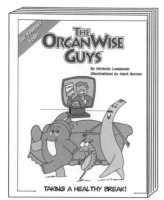

Taking a Healthy Break!

CALCI M. BONE®'S KIT:

My Favorite Drink in the World!

"Bone Bank" Savings!

A Teeth Changing Experience!

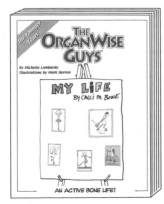

An Active Bone Life!

WINDY® THE LUNG'S KIT:

Clean Air March!

A Healthy Victory!

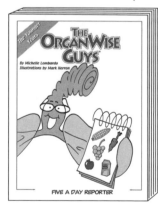

Five a Day Reporter

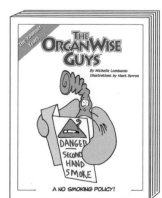

A No Smoking Policy!

HERE WE ARE!

Cut this page out on the dotted line. Color the four OrganWise Guys®. Using the labels below, trace the name for each of the characters. Using your best cutting skills, cut out each OrganWise Guy and the labels. Then glue or tape them in the correct place in the body outline on page 7.

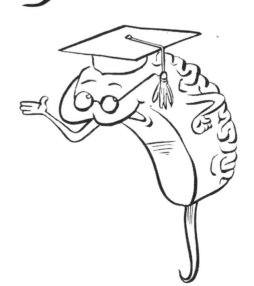

Hardy Heart

Madame Muscle

Sir Rebrum

Windy

PUT US WHERE WE LIVE

Using the picture on page 5 as your guide, glue or tape Sir Rebrum®, Hardy Heart®, Madame Muscle® and Windy®, the lungs in their correct location inside this body outline. Then place the correct label next to each character

BREAKFAST SENTENCES

Sir Rebrum® sure hopes you ate breakfast today. Now it's time for you to use your brain. Read each sentence.

Write a **.** at the end if it is a telling sentence.

Write a **?** at the end if it is an asking sentence.

Milk is healthy for your bones

Did you have milk with your breakfast

Have you ever had chocolate milk

Eggs come from chickens

Have you ever seen a real chicken

What color is the yolk of an egg

What is your favorite fruit

Monkeys like bananas

Orange juice is a healthy drink

Sir Rebrum will never skip breakfast again

Did you ever miss breakfast

Breakfast is the most important meal of the day

What is your favorite cereal

Write an asking sentence about breakfast. Give it to a friend to answer.

Did you ever miss breakfast

HEALTHY MATH

After Sir Rebrum® eats a good breakfast, he loves doing math. Read the story problem and write the correct answer in the box. Show your work.

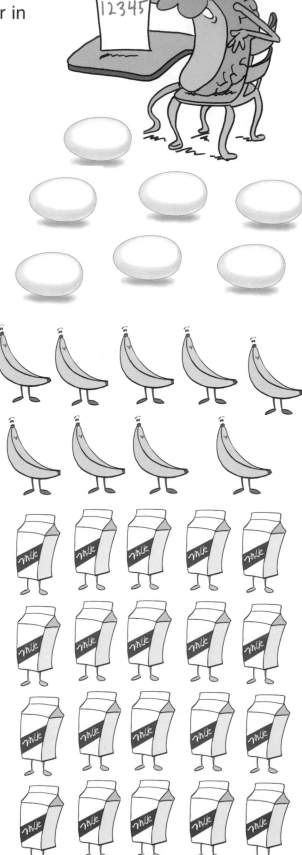

Sir Rebrum had 7 eggs. He made a good breakfast and ate two of the eggs. How many eggs were left?

Work and Answer

Hardy needs to bring 15 bananas to school for a party. He has 9 bananas at home. How many more bananas will he need to buy at the store on his way to school?

Work and Answer

Sir Rebrum helped serve breakfast in the school cafeteria. He started out with 20 cartons of milk. He handed out 1/2 of them during breakfast. How many did he have left?

Work and Answer

ALWAYS PUMPING

Hardy's job is to pump blood to every part of your body. Read and follow the instructions below.

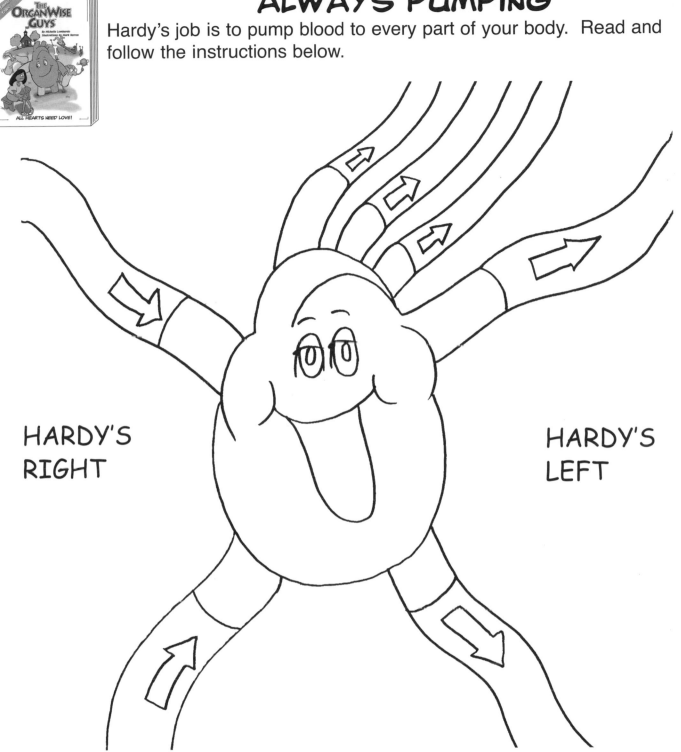

HARDY'S
RIGHT

HARDY'S
LEFT

1. Blood comes into Hardy on his **RIGHT** side. Color the two arteries **BLUE** that show the blood going into Hardy.

2. Blood gets pumped out of Hardy on his **LEFT** side. Color the five arteries **RED** that show the blood going out of Hardy.

3. Hardy is a healthy **PINK** color. Color him **PINK** with **BLUE** eyes.

BE KIND TO OTHERS

Hardy knows that being kind is a part of living a healthy life. Think of a time that you were kind to someone. Write about that time and how it made you feel. Then draw a picture of that time. Share your story with a friend.

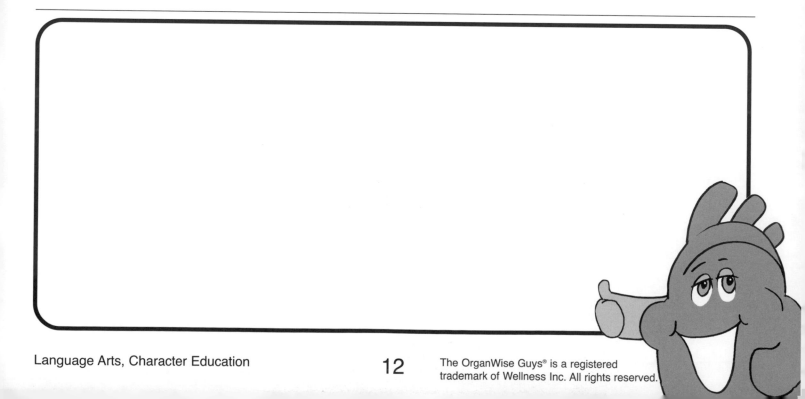

A HEALTHY COMMERCIAL

You have been chosen to star in a new "healthy television commercial" about eating more fruit. Pick one of the fruits shown below. Finish the script below of your "healthy commercial." Use your imagination and make it fun! Share with the class what you would say about that fruit.

bananas

apples

grapes

I love to eat _____.

I like this fruit because _____

_____.

I remember eating this fruit at _____

_____.

I think you should try this fruit. When you put it in your mouth it tastes like_____

_____.

Fruits taste great and are_____

_____.

Next time you want a snack be sure to _____

_____.

TURN OFF THE TV!

Hardy is serious about kids turning off the television. He wants you to get up and move around. He has made a crossword puzzle of physical activity words. Using the words below, fill in the puzzle so that each word fits correctly. (Hardy has filled in the first letter to get you started.) Then follow the directions below to finish the sentence.

tennis

walk

dance

run

exercise

football

Using the letters from the grey boxes, finish the sentence below.

An easy way to get physical activity is simply to go outside and have some ____ ____ ____!

CALCI'S FAVORITE DRINK!

Calci loves to write about milk. She needs you to help with this short paragraph.

Write a **1, 2, and 3** to show the order in which these sentences should appear in a paragraph.

____ Next, she gets a glass, pours a nice big glass of milk and drinks it.

____ First, Calci gets the milk out of the refrigerator.

____ Finally, she puts the milk back in the refrigerator and her empty glass in the dishwasher.

Write the sentences in order on the lines below to make a paragraph.

_____

_____

_____

_____

_____

_____

_____

_____

NEW MILK CARTONS

Calci has been asked to help make new milk cartons for a grocery store. She would like to hear some of your ideas. Below is the carton. She has also made a list of items that need to go on the carton. Design and color the carton by putting the items from her list and some of your own to make a milk carton that will get people's attention.

ITEMS FOR CARTON

Calci M. Bone

LOW-FAT MILK

GREAT FOR BONES!

BONE HEALTHY GRAPH

Calci asked students what their favorite "bone healthy, calcium-rich" food was. She colored in the graph for each of their answers. Read the graph she made. Answer the questions.

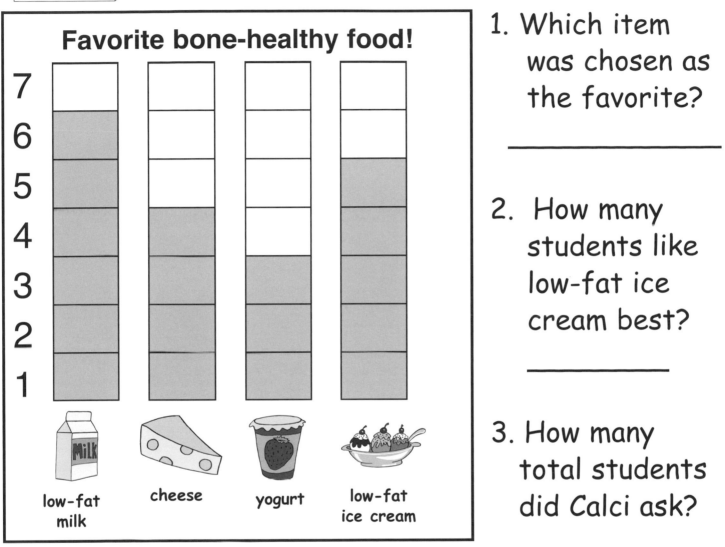

Favorite bone-healthy food!

7 6 5 4 3 2 1

low-fat milk   cheese   yogurt   low-fat ice cream

1. Which item was chosen as the favorite?

   _____

2. How many students like low-fat ice cream best?

   _____

3. How many total students did Calci ask?

   _____

4. How many students liked cheese and yogurt in total? _____

5. Which is your favorite item? _____

6. Color in the correct box on the graph to add your favorite to the total.

Math/Graphs, Nutrition

17

BONE HEALTHY SPENDING!

Calci M. Bone® has saved up some money for a "bone-healthy" shopping trip. Below is the money she is bringing with her. Help her choose what she should buy.

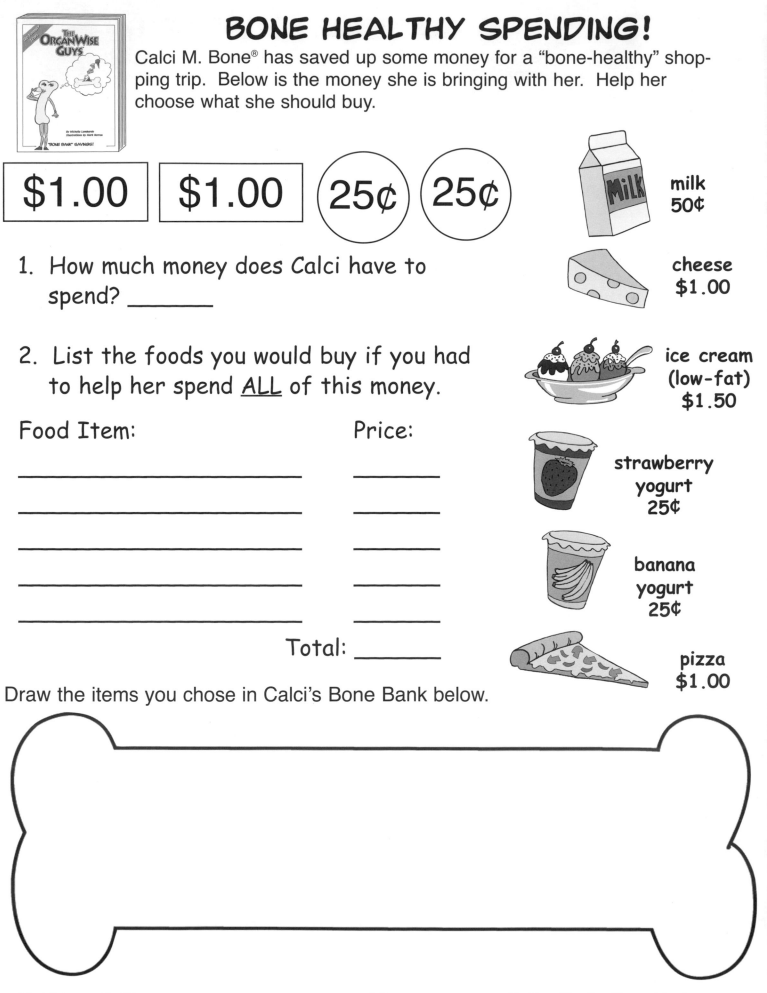

$1.00 $1.00 25¢ 25¢

milk 50¢

1. How much money does Calci have to spend? _____

cheese $1.00

2. List the foods you would buy if you had to help her spend **ALL** of this money.

ice cream (low-fat) $1.50

Food Item: Price:

_____   _____
_____   _____
_____   _____
_____   _____
_____   _____

Total: _____

strawberry yogurt 25¢

banana yogurt 25¢

pizza $1.00

Draw the items you chose in Calci's Bone Bank below.

A TEETH LESSON!

Listen to the story, "A Teeth Changing Experience." Write about your favorite part of the book and tell why you like it so much. Then draw and color a small illustration of that part in the circle below. Answer the question.

My favorite part!

_____

_____

_____

_____

_____

_____

What lesson did you learn from this story?

_____

_____

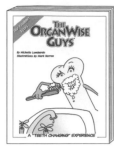

YOU BE THE ASSISTANT!

Pretend you are a dental assistant. Below is the inside of your patient's mouth who forgot to brush his teeth. They need your help. Design the toothbrush below for them. Make it colorful so they will want to use it a lot. Write a prescription telling your patient what needs to be done to keep their mouth healthy. Use the key words below in your prescription.

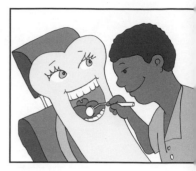

Key words

brush

morning

night

teeth

clean

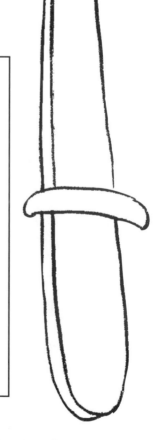

Healthy teeth presciption

Be sure to. . .

_____

_____

_____

_____

_____

YOUR ACTIVE LIFE

Read all of the ways that Calci M. Bone® stays active. Draw a picture of you in the snapshot below showing how you keep your bones strong with physical activity. Write a sentence about your picture.

baseball

basketball

karate

soccer

running

dance

gymnastics

hiking

jump rope

HEALTHY PROOFREADING!

Hardy has written an article for the school newspaper. He was in a hurry and forgot to check his spelling. He has misspelled 10 words. Put an X through each mis-pelled word and write the correct spelling above it. The first one has been done for you. Find the other nine. Then color the picture of Windy®.

Staying Smoke Free!

The "Clean Air ~~Macrh~~ March" was a big success. Windy the

lungs, and I had a great timme. We even made the

Sundae newspaper. At first, the march wuz kind of

small in size. But, once we beggan singing our "Clean

Air March" song the whole town cam out. Now every-

one wants to hepl keep our town healthy by staying

smook free. Next yeer when we

have the march, I sure hope you jion

in the fun!

Yours in good health,

Hardy Heart

STAY SMOKE FREE!

SERVING UP VEGGIES

Mr. Anthony wants you to come work at his "No Smoking" restaurant on Saturdays. Read the orders below and draw the pizza with the correct toppings. Then add up the total price of the pizza. Be sure to load them up with veggies for good health.

NO SMOKING

PIZZA SIZES

Large $7.00

Small $5.00

VEGGIE TOPPINGS

broccoli $1.00   tomatoes 50¢   onions 50¢   mushrooms $1.00

ORDER:	PRICE
Small Pizza	_____
broccoli	_____
onions	_____
Total:	_____

Your shift is over. Place and make a "to-go" pizza order for your family.

ORDER:	PRICE
_____	_____
_____	_____
_____	_____
_____	_____
_____	_____
Total	_____

ORDER:	PRICE
Large Pizza	_____
broccoli	_____
tomatoes	_____
mushrooms	_____
Total:	_____

Math, Life Skills, Nutrition

23

NO SMOKING POLICY!

One of Windy's goals is to help restaurant owners understand why it is so important to have a No Smoking policy. She needs you to help by writing a letter to a restaurant in your state convincing them to become a No Smoking one. Then design and color a No Smoking sign for them to use.

Dear Restaurant Owner,

_____

_____

_____

_____

_____

_____

_____

_____

Sincerely,

_____

P.S. Below is a "No Smoking" sign for you to display in your restaurant!

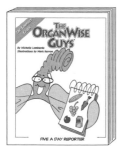

HEALTH REPORTER

As a health reporter you need to learn how to search out healthy hidden clues. Hidden in the park scene below are 10 pictures of the OrganWise Guys® and the 12 fruits and vegetables listed below. Find and circle all 22 of the hidden pictures.

- peas
- watermelon
- broccoli
- lemon
- bananas
- pineapple
- tomato
- cherries
- grapes
- corn
- pear
- carrot

ASSISTANT WRITER

Windy® needs help writing her article about all the fruits and vegetables that Hardy ate. Read along as your teacher reads the begining of her article. Using all of the items listed in Windy's notes, write about Hardy's day.

The mission was to see if Hardy Heart was eating enough fruits and vegetables. He ate more than 5 a day, hurray! Here is how his day went.

_____

_____

_____

_____

_____

_____

_____

_____

WINDY'S NOTES:

corn

banana

grapes

orange juice

apple

carrots

A SMART POLICY

Read the sentences below. Draw a line from the sentence to the picture that best describes that part of the "No Smoking Policy" story. Next, show the correct order of the story by writing 1,2,3 or 4 in the box next to each picture.

Anna's house now has a "No Smoking Policy." Grandma hugs Anna and promises to never smoke inside again!

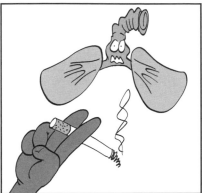

Anna ran outside to get away from the smoke.

Windy can't believe Grandma started smoking in the house.

Grandma made a healthy after-school snack.

Language Arts/Reading, Health

27

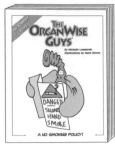

A VERY SPECIAL PERSON!

Anna just got a call from her Grandma saying that she is going to quit smoking for good. Anna is so proud of her! Think of a person you know who quit smoking or plans to quit smoking. Draw a picture of them in the box below. Write a few sentences telling them how proud you are of them for quitting or encouraging them to quit soon if they still smoke.

A Very Special Person

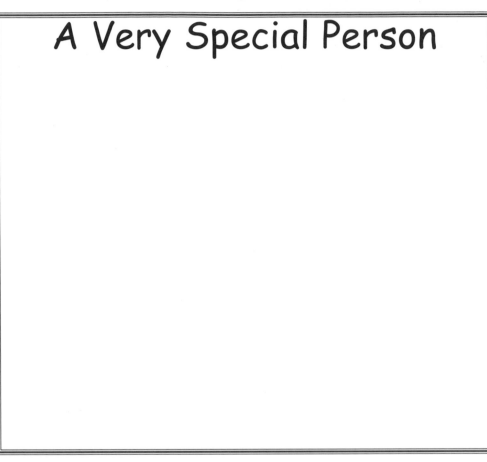

_____

_____

_____

_____

_____

_____

Lang. Arts, Character Ed., Health

28